Writing Rainbows

Poems for Grown-Ups

Richard Carl Subber

2017

First edition published in 2017.

This edition is self-published
by Richard Carl Subber, Natick, MA 01760

ISBN-13: 978-0-9986772-0-0
Library of Congress Control Number: 2017901928

Prepared in digital format or printed in hardcopy in the United States of America.

All named persons in my poems are fictitious.

Read more of my poems, book reviews and thoughtful commentary on my website:
http://richardsubber.com/

For additional copies of this book go to my website
or to Amazon and search for Richard Subber
or contact me: ricksubber@gmail.com

I am an experienced freelance editor and writing coach, with repeat clients in the US, Australia and Italy. Contact me so we can discuss how I can help you make your writing better.

My Facebook page:
https://www.facebook.com/authorRickSubber/
My LinkedIn profile:
www.linkedin.com/in/richardcsubber

gratias

My wife, Barbara, and my sister, Jan, have given me so much loving encouragement that has been essential in my writing, and in my re-writing, and in the joys of my life.

My thanks to Kimberly Hargis (WP Indiana, wpindiana.com). Kimberly created my website. I wrote these poems, and her design, technical, publishing, and marketing expertise made this book happen.

WP Indiana has 20 years of experience and specializes in WordPress, website and managed hosting for small business entrepreneurs, start-up businesses and home businesses.

Kimberly Hargis
WP Indiana
http://wpIndiana.com
khargis@outlook.com

Contents

Moment

It wasn't obviously a step-by-step process.
It seemed like it took years. It really was years.
A continuum of nights and days
and firsts and talking
and repeated joys
and the desperate acceptance of sickness
and the universe of smiles
and the glad warmth of wanton hugs
  and bodies that can touch everywhere, and do…

She grew, yet she's still so far from grownup,
still so completely the child you love,
but not a yearling,
  not a yearling.
Last night she murmured "I'm a little shy"
and you smiled a little, reassured her,
and crumbled a little, in your heart,
  it's one more fear you cannot fix…

Now she stands at your side,
calmly shouldering the backpack,
the totem of kindergarten.
You whisper, once, again, again,
  and she listens, she holds your hand.

Now she leans toward the big yellow bus,
the doors open wide—those steps are so high!—
and you kiss the back of her ear
as she leaves you standing alone,
  and takes the next step in her life.

September 19, 2016

Another 3rd grade tour

Well, yes, Anna, this is the same river
  the Natick Indians knew in 1651,
it was here, they fished in it,
and, yes, they saw ducks like those
  on the other bank over there,
and, no, it's not too deep,
but, here's another way to look at it:
the river is new today,
it's filled with new rain,
it carries a different twig over the dam,
it swirls new bubbles
  from the fish we didn't quite see,
the river has forgotten the feel of a canoe,
  forgotten how to turn the mill wheel,
it has learned to ignore
  the ever louder sounds that crowd the air,
and it sniffs in surprise
  each time new toes are dipped in its currents,
and those ducks on the other bank
  are new this year, too.

June 17, 2016

Lay me down

I ramble through the old pine woods, indulging the piney scents,
hearing again that these old stands—these old firs—make no noises,
trying again to make no unsettling sound.

The path opens wide, I take long views of spaces near and far,
on the left side, on the right side,
I see to darkness, and, I think, still farther to the almost seen,
to where tomorrow's further ramble may entice me to walk on.

The forest floor is everywhere, of course,
invisible in my span of sight and thought,
this moment, looking down, I see what had been naught.

I dare to say aloud in quiet words how wonderful
  to stand at ease on this endless blanket of such spartan weave
  and cushioned spread,
this muffling cloak of countless specks,
this yielding quilt of scarcely patterned brown,
this lingering layer of cast-off bits of these old trees
  that offer me at every step a bed of rest,
and a pillow of softest needles for my head.

September 18, 2015

It’s my move

Swing, my arms. Whirl me.
Touch my world, fingers. Make me feel.
Run, my legs. Move me.
   Take me somewhere.
See, my eyes. Yearn, my heart.
   Tempt me. Test me. Snare me.
      Make me content.
Then, turn, my feet. Take me home,
   but take a new road.

June 6, 2002

Dance in the night

Jittering dance of light and dark,
the jabs of motions,
frantic flow of hitch and start,
the dervish jolts, more dash and retreat,
more scuttle from the murky edge,
more hasty mash of shapes and lines,
they will not stay, they will not still,
they have no time to tarry.

These umbered sprites,
these shimmered dabs,
these moonstruck shadows of the credulous leaves
  that are tempted to live
    by the mischievous wind in the night.

September 15, 2015

Chant de mer

This sound, so hoarse and so huge,
the roiling water makes it a dimension,
boundless.

This sound, this frothing, thrumming, wordless
song of the sea,
this elemental sound, this tumbling burst from quiet deeps,
this very voice,
this prodigy of sound that needs no ear.

September 15, 2010

Numerology

He’s counting his fingers now,
  another threshold passed without a look back.
He puts some energy into it,
  doesn’t remember to count every one every time,
    but he’s counting, he’s doing it.

Old Grandfather starts it off,
  tapping fingertips, “One, two, three…”
  and he picks up the rhythm,
    splaying the fingers of one hand,
      fearlessly extending the count,
        “…four, five, seven, eight…”

A couple of those eager fingers get counted twice,
  sticking up like chicks in the nest
  stretching for the worm,
    and that’s alright, those fingers are stretching
    for the joy of discovery
    and the cool of flashing in the air
    in the ritual of counting fingers with Old Grandfather,
      and counting twice is confirmation, not a sin.

We do it again.
Same noisy delight. Different count.
Someday he’ll understand that doing it together is what counts.

October 10, 2015

Stone things

The stony silence in the great field
is a song whose words I do not hear,
  yet it beckons…
The stones have no voice
but their music rises from the resonant earth,
  a mix of ancient chords,
    the glacier's pulse for tempo.
The dull and dirty stones sing and sing,
  their harmony in millennial measure,
    their harmony in lasting sameness,
      each with each,
  and in their nature, enduring without change,
    without distinct past and future,
      with truth only in the moment,
perforce, with almost perfect resistance to change
in lieu of elegant quickening spirit.
These stones experience only place as variety,
  they are stone-like in whatever aspect,
    whatever place…

Their singing is a song of self, of steadfastness,
  of strongest will to be.
The stones do stone things wherever they may lie,
  in sheltering earth,
    or cast aside from a garden,
      in cairn, in wall—
the stones ever cling to their stony ways.

So. This is for learning.
I heed this clarion music of the stones
and I sing the song of me.
I cleave to my loves and my plans
and my special pleasures
and my sense of the right things,
  and yet I will welcome each new place
  and learn to be me there.

June 3, 2016

(Inspired by
"The Stones" in *New Collected Poems* by Wendell Berry)

Nova

"I pray you're not the devil."

Fears run skeltering through me,
thoughts come rushing, must I burn with blushing?

"Please don't make me get out of the car."

You bought my pies, I started when your smile
drew my gaze up to your eyes,
one quick breath—

"I'm….   I…."

I was the girl with the bonnet. Your fingers touched my hand,
your words were horizons, I felt the cymbal in my heart,
my breast pressed full inside my apron

"Don't hurt me. Take me with you."

I cannot think, I had no plan,
no impulse to resist your smile,
it beckoned me to cross a line,
it tore the thin cloak that pinned my arms
and wrapped my life

"I will be your woman."

....I don't know what those words mean.
Look at me.
I see a stranger in my body, a new spirit says my name,
new words boil in my brain,
this sudden dream jolts, this shaking...
I will not risk losing this chance to live,
I will not wait for another smile
to fill blank spaces in my life,
I will not wait until I have to say 'I could have but I didn't...'

"I will not be a girl with a bonnet."

September 9, 2015

O, patient sea

O, patient sea,
        wait for me.
I will always return.
I cannot forget the sea.
The constant sea will wait for me,
        I will always return.

The breaking sea o'erflows my view,
        it tumbles and splashes and glides to me,
                I will return to gaze anew.
I will return to face the sea.
O, patient sea,
        you need not wait for long for me.

September 16, 2008

Counting

A lonely hand reaches deep and wide.

Eleanor Rigby waits at the window—
I slump with full awareness
  that the window shuts her in,
her practiced sigh releases nothing
  to the farther side where
  hope could make a different noise.

The French girl twirls her rings
  and teases hopeful troth
  from the boy who learns too late
  she is too much for him,
the boy who will slump alone,
  later, at the café
  where her friends have
  no English words for him.

In like despair,
I shrink from such bandied silence
  that fills my ears and empties my heart,
I practice solitary sighs,
reaching deeper and wider
  for the touch
  that can tip the count to two.

January 18, 2017

(Inspired by
"Eleanor Rigby" [The Beatles, 1966]
"The French Girl" [Ian and Sylvia (Fricker) Tyson, 1966])

Listen

Surf sounds, *chansons de mer*,
the breaking rollers,
mellowed crunch of wave on wave,
the drumroll of eternal tides.

There is no silent sea, we think…

….consider a sheltered beach,
in the lee of a baffling sand bar,
sea-spawned shoal,
mediator for sea and shore,
muffler of the surf,
tamper of the bursting breakers,
damper of the singing of the sea,
guardian of truth about
the vastly silent blue water.

March 3, 2016

Après-midi des enfants

The pond's blue water, ruffling in precocious breezes,
coolly boiling with the thrashing and sparkly splashes
of sprites masquerading as children,
all enmeshed in the gentle net of watchful gazes,
all flaunting their carefree energy,
they tend to joy, they crave only more,
heedless of their unknown futures…

Rejoice, young and old!
The pond is now.

August 5, 2015

Understanding

There is much un-wisdom about the facts of being un-young:

The young may tend to un-imagine being un-young,
  the "o" word is mere input for them,
    an un-learned lesson.
The un-young may so clearly not un-see the truth,
  so eagerly not un-cherish youth as output, as sustenance,
    as resource, as co-reality.
The young have such tiny ideas about the "o" word.
We among the un-young do not un-recognize
  the broadening, erupting un-emptiness
    of childhood, of adolescence, of transition…
We do not un-cling to youngness.
We do not un-feel our youthful impulses that will not wane.
We do not un-gather children to our arms and our hearts.
We are not un-sure that youngness is not un-yoked to our living.
We cannot un-see that the young careen to their future,
  that they cannot come to un-know the 'o' word,
    that we may help them by un-hiding the possible,
      by linking their un-knowns to the un-ugliness
        we have made and not un-done.

Be un-doubtful about this.

November 9, 2015

Rite

It has a name, this unknown bloom,
and rightly would I use it,
but that certain naming is for another day.

Today I mark the color,
and the tinsel lattice of the flower heads
on clustered new growth.
I see the stark pattern of the thrusting stems
and tiniest petals,
the keen exotic profile of this beauty,
this sparing fan of sprites that cannot dance.
I raptly gaze at the sway and swoon
of this bounty,
this grant of nature,
this innocence—

I dare to give it yet another name.

July 7, 2016

"Sara from South Dakota"

You're the kid who yelled "I love the ocean!" the first time you saw it.
You're the little kid who didn't want to go back to the house for supper.

You're the kind of kid who won't stand still while Mom puts the lotion on.
You're the kind of kid who won't cry when the sunburn hurts.

You're the little girl who wanted to help that baby fill up her little blue bucket.
You would NOT let your brother help you build your castles.

You're the kid who doesn't want to go home to South Dakota " 'cause it's too far from the ocean, which is really fun."

You're the little kid who wasn't afraid to ask me "What's on the other side of the ocean?"…
    and you listened to my explanation, even though it was too long about other countries and other people,
    because you suddenly realized there are lots of places you haven't been to and you're pretty sure you want to go there,
    but it does seem a little scary…

You said "Thank you," and I guessed that I had taught you something.
You're young enough to be my granddaughter…
        maybe I'll have a granddaughter like you some day.

Later, at sundown, I saw that a child had written her name in the wet sand just below the high tide mark:

"Sara from South Dakota"

~~~~~~~~

with a squiggly line underneath.
I knew it was you.

You're the kind of kid who would do it.
You're the kind of kid who would say good-bye to the ocean.
That's a pretty big thing for a kid to do.

September 11, 2010
~~~~~~~~

Movin' on

I dream a new life…
my living here is not done,
but I am going.

May 16, 2014

Transition

My path, my crossings,
the trails I know, and my friends,
become memories…

May 9, 2014

Quo vadis?

familiar street—
its ripe comfort fades, recedes,
now I'm a stranger.

May 14, 2014

Taking leave

You hear it one time…
But many times, too many,
I say it: "last time"

May 23, 2014

…but I mean…

It hurts, this truth in
my heart: I say "goodbye" but
I mean "don't forget."

May 20, 2014

Going home

Waiting now, for that
"going home" feeling to come
back, come home, to me.

June 18, 2014

Lingering

The rain comes in, spattering, thin,
        staining high sand, sparing the lee.

Seabirds aloft, lifting, drifting,
        unhurried, as they scan the sea.

The rain comes in,
        then fades, silence,
                my delight is quiet in me.

July 8, 1991

(Revised with suggestions from Lindsay Smith)

Juncture

Mingled mist, mind.
Loosed vision, an impulse of the eye
        strains to see the lifting dawn,
                the shimmering dance of sunrise.

Surrounding sound peals the senses,
I whirl and stretch to the horizon, a stroke in air,
the great broad sky beyond my reach,
I dip one toe and the ocean swallows me entire.

Undeniable, ineffable world outside my world.

June 24, 1995

Baptism

He launches his small body forward in space, from the edge of the pool, ignorant of gravity, heedless of the deep water and the elemental danger.

He plunges in, grinning.

He rises, gulping air, laughing, in his father's arms.

He cannot know what a father may fear.

He cannot know that Daddy lurches with instinctive frenzy to grab him every time he jumps.

He cannot know that his dad's proud shouts of approval mask the primal imperative to shout "Be careful, son!"

He cannot know that a father's love drives the ritual: to teach jumping, to expose the underwater mysteries, to stand chest-deep in the pool and urge a beloved son to risk his life with every jump.

He cannot know that, at some future time, when the time is right, he himself will ignore his guardian duty, and eagerly, with a smile, beckon to his own child to make the first intrepid leap.

August 22, 2015

Heart burn

You taught me to yearn,
I was so ready to learn.
Oh!....so full of you.

March 28, 2015

Evensong

The owl, that one call,
quickens my longing to sing
only one note, mine.

April 4, 2015

Another lesson

La fleur blanche, its scent
a gift, so gently teaching
my heart how to give.

March 27, 2016

I have listened

I think I want to
say some words you didn't hear
when you were talking.

I think I want to
say out loud what other folks
will only whisper.

I think I want to
write a story no one can
hear without my ears.

July 20, 2015

Seeing far…

I hope Aunt Cam knew we were there today.

It's a delicate hope,
  less desperate than it is urgent,
    less spiritual than it is personal,
      private, protective….

It is my fragile awareness that I imagine
  the searing loneliness of dying without
    the careful press of fingers touching me,
      the caressing hands of my loved ones
        who want to be sure the touch is special, warm…

I want to know they will surround me
  when my time comes,
    I want to believe I will know they are near,
      I want to know for sure I will hear them
        even if I cannot wake…

I realize I am saying,
  with great love and with profound selfishness,
    I hope Aunt Cam knew we were there today.

August 30, 2012

Horse sense

Nothing was changed, really.
The long placid pasture sprawled in the sun.
Horses studded the far slope,
  heads down, cropping the wasted offering of autumn time,
    all still in the moments of my passing.
A tableau in the periphery on all those other days,
  but yesterday I turned and looked far, saw more.
Yesterday I came to my senses.
In those long moments,
  I was a lover of horses.

November 12, 2015

Always…

I
will
be your
trusted friend,
always care for you.

I
will
walk your
path in life,
always there for you.

I
will
feel your
joys and hurts,
always share with you.

March 18, 2015

Drifters

Holding hands, we drift to dreams and easy sleep,
our touching is a grace of love, this long embrace is ours to keep.

September 6, 2015

First words

He's in full voice, it fills the ear,
the sounds of love are what we hear.

September 6, 2015

The ringing

The children laughing,
and sounding their chimes of mirth,
new peals of young joy.

October 12, 2016

Raptor

Quick to beat, you glide, explore,
  you rise and fall on shearing currents,
    clearing through,
      you fill a moving space in air.

You soar,
  and that's not all you do.

July 6, 2015

River talk

Roll on, you burly river,
  roil, run, in jumbling eddies,
    in dervish currents,
  in mute frenzy,
    potent, *puissant*, *dominante*,
roll on, you burly river.

April 9, 2014

Impedimenta

I open my mind to poetic whimsies,
  but the clatter of the TV voices
  makes it hard to listen to
  the other spirits who fill the ether,
    who strive to call, each to each,
      and to me.

I open my eyes to new vistas
beyond my familiar view,
  but the dervish clutter of dancing logos
  and streaming headlines
  and indulgently obscure commercial images
  makes it hard to see clearly
  the protean scenes
  that may ripen my life.

The beguiling screen fades to dark.

I breathe in, deeply…

I'm wide open.

August 23, 2016

Zephyr

A sterling breeze, a
soughing strum, a smooth caress,
a spare, splendid grace.

Aug 19, 2014

Take your time

Do you remember that tender time
when your little feet stumbled as you walked the sand,
  and you leaned against the sea breeze to stay upright
  as you imagined you would take the ocean in your stride?

September 18, 2015

Vanity

Is it too hard to do the right thing?
Is it right to do the hard thing?

We feel old passion to stand up
and stand fast,
  in our crystal rectitude,
    for the right thing.
We know it, we love it,
  it is a thriving joy,
    manifest in our minds
    and in my hearts.

The mighty do not marvel.
The minions are not moved.
Other multitudes will not make
a murmur to urge us
to dream of good works,
  they do not encourage yearning
  to do the public good that slights no man.

Our prospect is more vain striving,
  or the meaner choice:
  endorse a pale type of the right thing.

The hard work—
the imperative reach for some right portion—
is to make our halloo to a lesser incarnation
of this dream that will not live in other hearts.

March 11, 2016

The idea of the Grand Canyon

None but Colossus could stand at the brink and think “river valley.”

We don’t have ready words
  for a wholly identifiable place whose reality overflows sensation,
    whose dimension exceeds all power to estimate,
      whose magnitude has no analog,
        whose unseen shapes have no scalable size…
No one has ever stepped back from the rim and said “it reminds me of…”

This canyon is so real and so huge,
  the mind strains to grasp its emptiness, its nothingness,
    strains to believe the creator river is so small.

This canyon, this downward lofting cleft in earth,
  this shrine of birth,
    this canyon exists, unaware…
      it awaits perceiving intelligence…

A mind awaits, a gasping, gaping mind awaits
  to conceive the canyon’s unsayable beauties.
Two eyes await to look wide, and look deep.

October 23, 2015

The boy with a red hat

Just a little boy playing on the beach?
Him?
No. He is a dreamer, making his mark.

Skinny legs pumping as he navigates the sand,
Dad's big red hat on his head,
  pinched in behind so it fits,
    the big brim points his way,
      his eyes are hidden…
      but his vision is clear.

He announces to his Dad that the task is "building cities."
        He is the Designer,
          he is the Engineer,
            he is the Sand Hauler,
              he is the Shovel Handler,
                he is the Bucket Man,
                  he is the Creative Force.

A little boy playing in the sand?
No. He is a city builder.

September 17, 2008

(Revised with suggestions from Lindsay Smith)

Solo

Once more I come,
again I hear
the lashing surf,
the endless thrum.

Once more I gaze,
again, delight
to see so far
and taste salt haze.

Once more I'm blessed:
the zephyr's lull,
the rasp of sand,
O! sea! O! zest!

July 2013

A simple pirouette

I see her, a child dancing on the sand,
  as my child once was—
    I see him again—
  I almost see the ample sand with a child's eyes.
Once I was a child on the sand.

My memory spans the years,
  simply bridged by gazing at this child in her simple pirouette,
    her moment, she surges gaily now, in her turn.

A simple cycle, the recurring rhythm,
  the carefree whirl, the blossom of delight—
all quickening my wistful gaze…

July 14, 1998

As the gull sees it

The sea is inches deep,
I do not heed the moving mountain of the surf,
it ceases tumbling far from me,
I do not hear it, do not lurch to meet it.

The sand is vast, I see no marks but my own,
the prints of sandaled feet so large they make no shape for me,
only outlines of space I do not need.

The sky is my domain but, in truth,
I need small air above my feeding range,
small air above my nightly refuge—
sky-wide and sky-tall are words I do not need.

The long view to the horizon has no dream for me,
the boundary of sky is no limit,
the edge of sea is no temptation.

My world is small, I fill it,
and I am larger than my shadow,
as I see it.

September 15, 2015

Real enough

The kids move easily in imaginary worlds.
They conjure the details as needed,
  and repeat them to me
  to confirm what must be real right now.
They don't need many details,
  the facts are simple,
    the yin and the yang are vivid.
The bad monkeys have no masks,
  the good monkey catchers have the kids' faces
  and they have super powers too,
    powers so vast, potent, inspired by the urgency
    of good crushing evil,
      every power springs from the end of the mighty sword
      that looks like a wrapping paper tube in different light.
The kids move easily in imaginary worlds
where sufficient reality can be summoned,
  and outcomes are fixed,
    and there is only valor and virtue and victory.

January 9, 2016

(Inspired by
The Philosophical Baby by Alison Gopnik)

Tree verses

Tree?

Art thou a tree?
Maybe so.

Metal?

Art? Thou a tree?
May be. So?

Metal tree.

Art thou? A tree,
maybe. So.

September 20, 1993

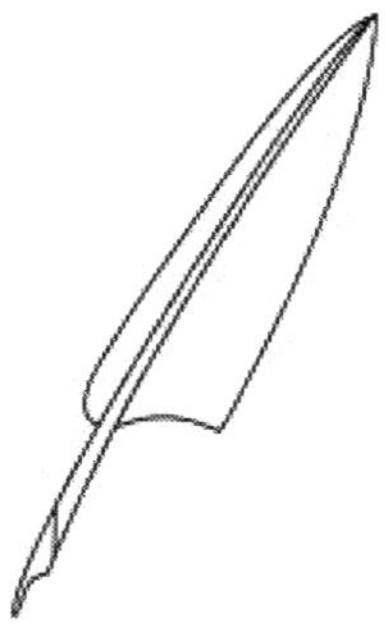

Another look

I think it's true that you can't stand still
on railroad tracks without thinking about
going somewhere,
  especially if you're alone,
    in an old cut,
and you feel a chill in the air
and the tracks are cold, you touch one rail,
  it isn't shiny any more,
    the last train through maybe was a milk run
    with a steam engine, no one remembers…

You wait to take a step
because it seems easier to wait
a few moments more,
  because you can't stop staring down the tracks
  and you can't tell if you're looking ahead
  or looking to the past...will you go
  on to a new dream,
    or maybe head back
    to something you didn't want to leave?

Maybe it's different if you're not alone.

August 15, 2016

largo

Come.
Abide with me.
We know enough
to sit, content,
   not even a word between us.
No need to speak,
   we mutely share our delight
   at day's end in
   our accustomed bower.

A pattering rain comes and goes,
   the shower scents remain,
      and lingering drops escape
      from drooping leaves,
         to make a different silence,
and we have time to listen.

May 19, 2016

(Inspired by
"One Way to Spend an Afternoon Together" by Rosemerry Wahtola Trommer)

Sounding

In the remnant of today
I stand, silent, separate,
  satisfied that I have filled
  my space and my time well enough
  in this diurnal turn.

A bit of travel, something of travail,
  but I am bold
  and I pushed through.

My journey wide, and ventures far,
  I sounded deep this day.
I dared to laugh,
  I shrank from dread,
    I tasted new spice of living,
      I wrapped my arms around my love,
        and now I welcome night.

I'll dream awakening to a new path,
  a new slope,
    I'll incline to try it in another turning.

March 1, 2016

On finding a shell at Bethany Beach

Survivor among a multitude.
Ravaged. Elegant. Incomplete.

A wreck of life,
  a silent ambush of the eyes.

Stoop to it, be wise,
  see the wonder in your hand.

Hold it,
          take it.
Leave your footprint in the sand.

(Written at Bethany Beach, Delaware)
May 23, 1993

Still time

Swirled mists lingering on the fen,
a layered cloak of fleecing, fleeting airs,
a pale disguise that hides almost nothing,
a mystic moment that slips away.

November 5, 2015

Snooze

Trying to hold back wakefulness
is all too easy,
  the conspirators will not be denied.
Eyelids all too ready
to pretend the dawn has dallied,
  shoulders softly angled down,
    ready for a covering weight
    and nothing more,
  arms that will not reach high,
    only shifting, grasping seekers
    of the pillow,
      the huggy pillow.

My wakeful spirit that would rush
to delight in day, in duty,
  in daring to pile up the victories
  and run out the clock—
this day that spirit has lost a round,
  and must abide,
    while I recline and slumber
    and hug the squishy pillow,
      just a little longer.

April 7, 2016

Debut

Saucy streaks in brightened sky at dawn
frame enlightened trees on yonder sward.
The arching hues quickly pale
to common blues,
   and slide below still darkened earth,
      beneath the rim that hides
      the great star of day.

March 13, 2016

Remembrances
(*Je me souviens*)

Airs and airs, brisking through the afternoon,
fill my ears with ruffling sound,
and fully charge my mind with half-drawn shapes,
many half-thought fancies,
and many second memories
   of once-remembered moments in the afternoon.

September 18, 2015

To Marcela

Your life has so many promises for you,
  so many doors will open for you.
May you pass through the portal of love,
  and never look back!
Your life will be separate from our lives,
you will travel roads we will not know,
you will sing songs we will not hear,
you will listen in some silences
  we will not imagine...

Your living here with us is done,
but we're not done with you.
Your living here has filled our hearts,
your tender touch lingers
  on the cheeks of the kids,
your smiles abide in every room.

No te olvidaremos.

Nov 28, 2016

Chanson de mer

I am the rock.
I am the island.
I am the glistening boulder at the waterline.
I am the sharp-edged, flinty fragment,
  tossed by the blue-green surge,
    scattered by the stinging wind,
      collected once, and dropped, by a child.
I am the ancient stratum exposed to the faintly salty air.
I am the blunt face of the heaved-up, broken stone,
  I am the silent witness to the everlasting crash and song of the sea,
    I stand against the tumbling, roiling crests that
                dash to me,
        break on me,
                climb my height,
        die at my foot,
                and rise, vaulting, surging, crashing, singing,
        to grandly break on me again, again…
        the lyric, rhythms, chords the same as at the last or next
millennial dawn.
I am the rock, the sea endlessly sings to me.
Good. Enough.
Tarry.
Listen.

Sep 15, 2011

Essence

The complex rapture of the sunset,
  the burdened bloom of the view on the great ridge,
    the spiraling sense of prismed mystery
    as the eye invades the glinting pool:
here is girth and span beyond our frame,
  vigor beyond our doing,
    beauty beyond our ken,
      life beyond our knowing.
We share all this space and time with the stones and the creatures
  and the waters of the earth and the cycles of the luminous skies
    and the skittering leaves and the bones of the dead.
These are existences which proceed and persist with us,
  against us and without us.
We indulge our myths that we are the odd lot, the specials, the self-chosen…
...perchance, we understand that we need the very stones
  and the creatures and the waters of the earth
    and the cycles of the luminous skies of the days and the nights,
      and the skittering leaves
        and the very bones of all the dead.

December 26, 2015

Read more of my poems, book reviews and thoughtful commentary on my website:
http://richardsubber.com/

For additional copies of this book go to my website
or to Amazon and search for Richard Subber
or contact me: ricksubber@gmail.com

I am an experienced freelance editor and writing coach, with repeat clients in the US, Australia and Italy. Contact me so we can discuss how I can help you make your writing better.

My Facebook page:
https://www.facebook.com/authorRickSubber/

My LinkedIn profile:
www.linkedin.com/in/richardcsubber

Publication Credits

The Aurorean

Walk this way	accepted for Spring/Summer 2017 issue

The Australia Times Poetry

It's my move	October 23, 2015
Lay me down	August 12, 2016
Listen	December 18, 2015 (earlier version)
Nova	September 11, 2015
Numerology	May 6, 2016
Stone things	November 18, 2016
Understanding	February 12, 2016

miller's pond

Lay me down	April 6, 2016
Numerology	February 13, 2016
Rite	September 4, 2016

Northern Stars

Juncture	November 18, 2016
Raptor	December 12, 2015
River talk	December 12, 2015

Whispers

Always…	March 18, 2015
Another 3rd grade tour	July 29, 2016
Dance in the night	January 3, 2016
Drifters	September 20, 2015
First words	September 20, 2015

It's my move	November 12, 2015
Juncture	September 20, 2015
Lingering	May 21, 2015 (as "The rain comes in")
Listen	March 2, 2016 (earlier version)
Numerology	May 5, 2016
O, patient sea	July 17, 2015
The ringing	December 15, 2016
"Sara from South Dakota"	September 2, 2016

The RavensPerch

Après-midi des enfants	March 8, 2016

Creative Inspirations

Après-midi des enfants	November 15, 2016
…but I mean…	May 10, 2015
Chant de mer	July 6, 2015
Evensong	November 14, 2015
Going home	May 10, 2015
It's my move	July 2, 2016
Lingering	February 28, 2016
Movin' on	September 8, 2015
O, patient sea	May 13, 2016
Quo vadis?	September 8, 2015
Seeing far…	March 1, 2015
Taking leave	May 10, 2015
Transition	September 8, 2015

41324164R00035

Made in the USA
Middletown, DE
09 March 2017